ANIMALS ON THE BRINK

Kangaroos

Patricia Miller-Schroeder

MEDIA ENHANCED BOOKS
AV²
BY WEIGL™
ADDED VALUE · AUDIO VISUAL

www.av2books.com

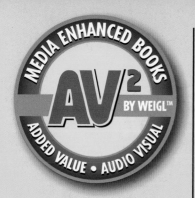

MEDIA ENHANCED BOOKS
AV²
BY WEIGL™
ADDED VALUE • AUDIO VISUAL

AV² provides enriched content that supplements and complements this book. Weigl's AV² books strive to create inspired learning and engage young minds in a total learning experience.

Your AV² Media Enhanced books come alive with...

Audio
Listen to sections of the book read aloud.

Key Words
Study vocabulary, and complete a matching word activity.

Video
Watch informative video clips.

Quizzes
Test your knowledge.

Go to **www.av2books.com**, and enter this book's unique code.

Embedded Weblinks
Gain additional information for research.

Slide Show
View images and captions, and prepare a presentation.

BOOK CODE
L209214

Try This!
Complete activities and hands-on experiments.

... and much, much more!

AV² by Weigl brings you media enhanced books that support active learning.

Published by AV² by Weigl
350 5th Avenue, 59th Floor
New York, NY 10118
Website: www.av2books.com   www.weigl.com

Library of Congress Cataloguing in Publication data available upon request.
Fax 1-866-449-3445 for the attention of the Publishing Records department.

ISBN 978-1-62127-226-7 (hardcover)
ISBN 978-1-62127-227-4 (softcover)

Printed in the United States of America in North Mankato, Minnesota
1 2 3 4 5 6 7 8 9 17 16 15 14 13

032013
WEP300113

Project Coordinator Aaron Carr
Design Mandy Christiansen

Every reasonable effort has been made to trace ownership and to obtain permission to reprint copyright material. The publishers would be pleased to have any errors or omissions brought to their attention so that they may be corrected in subsequent printings.

Photo Credits
Weigl acknowledges Getty Images as its primary photo supplier for this title.

Contents

Take a Stand
Debate • Research

How to take a stand on an issue   **5**

Should the Australian
government ban the sale
of kangaroo meat and
other products?   **17**

Is it acceptable to remove
problem animals in order
to save kangaroos?   **23**

Should the Australian
government allow the
taking of surplus kangaroos?   **31**

The Kangaroo

When people think of Australian animals, they often think of kangaroos or koalas. Both kangaroos and koalas belong to a group of animals called marsupials. Marsupials give birth to young that are not fully formed. These newborns must grow and develop for many months before they can live apart from their mother. Many marsupials, such as the kangaroo, carry their young in a pouch until they become fully developed.

In this book, you will meet kangaroos that are no larger than a rat and others that were thought to be **extinct**. You will discover that some kangaroos live in trees, while others live in rock piles. You will learn how some kangaroos can live in deserts so dry that there is no water for most of the year. You will also discover how a young kangaroo seeks protection in its mother's pouch when danger arises.

In Australia, kangaroos are often informally referred to simply as "roos."

Fur color varies among kangaroos. Some have very dark fur, while others may be almost white.

How to Take a Stand on an Issue

Research is important to the study of any scientific field. When scientists choose a subject to study, they must conduct research to ensure they have a thorough understanding of the topic. They ask questions about the subject and then search for answers. Sometimes, however, there is no clear answer to a question. In these cases, scientists must use the information they have to form a hypothesis, or theory. They must take a stand on one side of an issue or the other. Follow the process below for each Take a Stand section in this book to determine where you stand on these issues.

1. **What is the Issue?**
   a. Determine a research subject, and form a general question about the subject.

2. **Form a Hypothesis**
   a. Search at the library and online for sources of information on the subject.
   b. Conduct basic research on the subject to narrow down the general question.
   c. Form a hypothesis on the subject based on research to this point.
   d. Make predictions based on the hypothesis. What are the expected results?

3. **Research the Issue**
   a. Conduct extensive research using a variety of sources, including books, scientific journals, and reliable websites.
   b. Collect data on the issue and take notes on all information gathered from research.
   c. Draw conclusions based on the information collected.

4. **Conclusion**
   a. Explain the research findings.
   b. Was the hypothesis proved or disproved?

Kangaroo
Connections

Large kangaroos hop at 40 miles (64 kilometers) per hour. This is faster than a racehorse can run.

A male gray kangaroo holds the record for distance, jumping 44 feet (13.4 meters) in a single leap.

Features

The continent of Australia is very large and has many different **habitats** in which animals live. Kangaroos have developed special features that help them survive in these varied habitats. Some types of kangaroos live in dry areas, such as the vast, open Outback that covers much of Australia. These animals have features that help them conserve water. Other types of kangaroos live in forests and need to climb trees or hide in bushes to avoid **predators**. Some kangaroos have features that help them travel on rock piles as safely as mountain goats.

Yet, all kangaroos share some of the same special features. All kangaroos are marsupials and carry their young in pouches. Scientists call kangaroos macropods because they have big feet. In Greek, *macro* means "large" and *pod* means "foot." Kangaroos travel on two sturdy hind legs, usually by hopping.

Different types of kangaroos range from large to small. Small kangaroo **species**, such as the rat kangaroo, weigh less than 2 pounds (0.9 kilograms). The red kangaroo is the largest species. Males of this species can stand more than 7 feet (2.1 meters) tall and weigh 200 pounds (90 kg). There are major size differences between males and females in many of the large kangaroo species, such as the red and gray kangaroos. Females may be only half the size of males. Kangaroos grow throughout their lives, which means that the largest males are also the oldest.

No matter how large kangaroos grow, they all start life as very small creatures. Large species of kangaroos have tiny newborns that are only about three-quarters of an inch (1.9 centimeters) long. This is the size of a large bee.

Kangaroos are **mammals**. Like other mammals, their bodies are covered with hair or fur. Newborn kangaroos are pink and hairless. Their fur grows as they develop in the pouch. By the time they are between 3 and 6 months of age, the skin of most species is covered by a fur coat. Many kangaroos are shades of blue, gray, or red, but some are black, yellow, or brown.

The average life span for a kangaroo living in nature is 6 or 7 years. Some kangaroos, however, can live to be about 20 years old. Old kangaroos face the problem of how long their teeth last. A kangaroo's molar teeth wear out from eating tough plant food and are replaced one at a time. The molars grow in the back of the mouth and slowly move forward. By the time one tooth wears out, it has reached the front of the mouth and falls out. A new molar takes its place. The limit for tooth replacement is 16 molars. If an old kangaroo runs out of teeth, it may die because it cannot eat.

Classification

Kangaroos belong to the large **order** of mammals called Diprotodontia, or marsupials. While some marsupials live in South America, New Guinea, and islands surrounding Australia, most types live in Australia. There are thought to be at least 54 species of kangaroos. Experts do not always agree on exactly how many species there are. Some species are very rare, and some have been discovered in just the past few years.

The Macropodidae family, sometimes called true kangaroos, includes the largest and best-known types of kangaroos. The red kangaroo, or *Macropus rufus*, the eastern gray kangaroo, or *Macropus giganteus*, and the western gray kangaroo, or *Macropus fuliginosus*, are some of them. Most of the species in this family look very similar. Size is the main difference among the species. True kangaroos live in a variety of habitats, from deserts, **scrubs**, and open plains to woodlands and moist forests. Members of the Macropodidae family usually eat grasses and leaves. Wallaroos, wallabies, and tree kangaroos are smaller members of this family. Members of the Potoroidae family of marsupials are related to true kangaroos. They include several small species, such as musky rat kangaroos, potoroos, and bettongs.

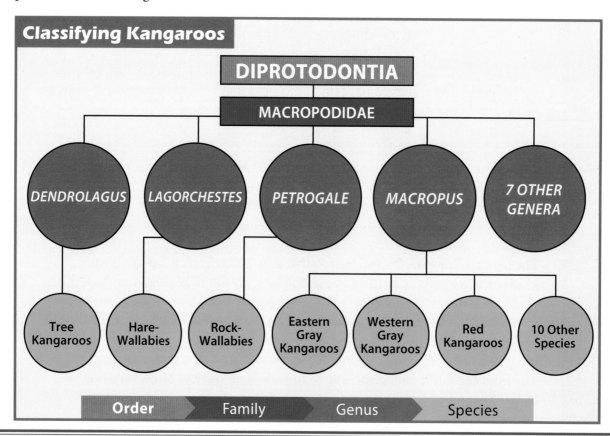

Classifying Kangaroos

DIPROTODONTIA

MACROPODIDAE

DENDROLAGUS · LAGORCHESTES · PETROGALE · MACROPUS · 7 OTHER GENERA

Tree Kangaroos · Hare-Wallabies · Rock-Wallabies · Eastern Gray Kangaroos · Western Gray Kangaroos · Red Kangaroos · 10 Other Species

Order → Family → Genus → Species

Tree kangaroos, which are small to medium-size animals, spend most of their time living in trees. They have stronger front legs than larger types of kangaroos. This helps them to climb.

The yellow-footed rock-wallaby is very agile and can jump from rock to rock.

The red kangaroo is the largest pouch-bearing mammal in the world.

Special Adaptations

Kangaroos are **herbivores**. They eat a wide range of grasses and other plants. Most kangaroos are nocturnal, which means they rest during the day and are active at night. They spend most of their active time eating. To get from place to place, kangaroos move in a way that is unique to macropods. They hop, with both feet pushing off the ground at the same time. Kangaroos have many other special features that help them to survive in their natural environment.

Teeth and Jaw

Kangaroos have a space behind their front teeth where they form plant material into wads. These wads of tough plant material are then ground up by the animal's molars. The lower jaw is made of two bones that can separate so that the jaw spreads to make room for more food.

Feet

The kangaroo's hind feet are long and thin, providing a springboard from which to push off for each leap. Most kangaroos have four toes on each hind foot. Each toe has a sharp claw. The middle toe is especially long and does much of the work when pushing into a jump. This toe is also used as a weapon.

Ears

Kangaroos have large ears like those of a deer. The ears can be turned in all directions and can pick up sounds from great distances. This helps to warn kangaroos of any approaching danger.

Legs

Kangaroo hind legs are large and powered by strong muscles. Even when kangaroos are standing still, their legs are ready to hop. Once a kangaroo gets going, it can hop for a long time without tiring. When necessary, the largest kangaroos can jump over 10-foot (3-m) fences from a standing position.

Tail

The kangaroo's tail is almost as long as the rest of its body and is loaded with muscles. The tail is important in helping the kangaroo keep its balance. It also helps the kangaroo walk by providing support, like an extra leg.

Kangaroo
Connections

Although kangaroos generally pose no threat to humans, large kangaroos, especially males, can be dangerous. If they are harassed or cornered, they can use their hind legs and claws to cause serious injury.

A large kangaroo can balance its entire body weight on its tail when fighting.

Groups

The kind of environment an animal lives in affects how it interacts with others in groups. Kangaroo social life is affected by whether the climate is dry or wet, what food and shelter are available, and which predators are a threat. Some types of kangaroos are very social, while others live alone.

Most kangaroos live in groups ranging in size from two or three to about 50. The large kangaroos, such as reds, grays, and some of the larger wallabies, often gather in very large groups. These groups are called **mobs**. For kangaroos, there is safety in numbers. In large, open areas, a mob has more eyes and ears with which to detect predators. Kangaroos living in mobs have less chance of being picked out of the group by predators and eaten.

Most kangaroo mobs have five times as many females as males. Adult females, which are called does, usually have young kangaroos, called joeys, with them. Many females in a mob are related. Adult males, which are called boomers, compete with other males for the females. A very strong, old male is called the old man. The old man is **dominant** when it comes to getting food, shade, or mates, but he does not really lead or protect the group.

Kangaroos also have groups within the mob that they usually associate with more, like having close friends. These kangaroos spend more time grazing, grooming, and resting together than with other members of the mob. They remain in sight of the rest of the mob for protection, however.

Some of the smaller kangaroos, such as quokkas, live in loose family groups, with one male collecting a few females. Other small kangaroos, such as hare-wallabies, live alone. A usual group consists of only a mother and a joey.

Male kangaroos, especially those of the larger species, challenge each other to test their strength. They do this by **sparring**, in what often looks like a boxing match. Two males rear up on their hind feet and try to push each other off balance. They may jab at each other with their forefeet or lock forelegs as they try to push each other over. They usually throw their heads back to protect their eyes from being scratched. If neither male backs down, the fight may become more intense. Usually, the males do not injure each other unless the fight turns very serious. Young male kangaroos start to practice play-sparring at an early age, wrestling with their mothers. They may push her with their front paws and try to knock her over with their hind legs.

Kangaroo
Connections

Kangaroos have a habit of hopping away quickly from danger and then stopping to look around. This can make them an easy target for human hunters with guns.

Today's kangaroos probably descended from small rat-sized marsupials that lived in trees about 25 million years ago.

Communication

Kangaroos, like other animals, have a variety of ways to communicate with one another. They may glance or hiss at each other. As a way of greeting, they approach and carefully sniff each other's nose. Kangaroos also kick, jab, punch, and touch. When there is danger, they alert one another by thumping their feet loudly and banging their tails on the ground. The members of the mob then scatter to get away from the source of danger.

One important way that kangaroos communicate is through **vocalizations**. Kangaroos are quiet communicators. Even when frightened, excited, or angry, they do not make loud howls, screams, or snarls. Their vocalizations are softer, like coughs or hisses.

Vocalizations occur during fights or sparring matches between males, when grunts and clicks can be heard. Males may then use coughing sounds to signal that they want to back away from a fight. Both red and gray kangaroos can make a low growling noise when they are annoyed.

Vocalizations also occur between mothers and their joeys. When joeys are big enough to venture out of their mothers' pouches, red kangaroo mothers call them back with clicking sounds. Gray kangaroo mothers do the same thing with clucking sounds. If danger is present, the joey quickly jumps back into the pouch. Kangaroo mothers also communicate with their offspring through grooming behavior. Adult kangaroos may also groom one another, using their paws, claws, and tongue.

From an Expert

"Tourists should see kangaroos in the wild, but instead they see them in a zoo or dead by the side of a road. If we can find areas with large kangaroo populations and develop them properly, kangaroos will become a positive tourist attraction."
- David Croft

David Croft is a former teacher at the University of New South Wales. He is one of Australia's foremost experts on kangaroo behavior and biology.

Body Language

Kangaroos use their bodies to send signals to each other and to other animals. These signals include foot thumping, kicking, punching, glancing, touching, sniffing, and grooming. Kangaroos may also use signals that scientists do not yet recognize.

Aggression

When two male kangaroos are interested in the same female as a mate, they often spar with their front legs. They may also balance on their tails and kick out with both hind legs. Kangaroos may also bite and use the sharp claws on their hind feet. A kangaroo usually does this only when it is faced with a major challenge from another kangaroo or has to defend itself against a predator such as a **dingo**.

Distress

When kangaroos sense that a threat is present, they show their distress by thumping their large hind feet. This signal always gets attention from others in the group. When the thumping signal is heard, joeys head for their mothers' pouches, and the whole mob scatters. In addition, when young kangaroos are separated from their mothers, they huddle closely together until they are found.

Mating

When a male senses that a female is ready to mate, he may sniff her pouch, scratch her tail, and rub his head along her back. If another male is interested in the same female, he challenges the first male to a sparring match until one of them backs down.

Closeness

Kangaroos groom one another as a sign of closeness and friendliness. When grooming, they lick and comb their own fur and the fur of others. They use their tongues and sharp front claws. They also use two hind toes that are joined together to form a grooming claw. Although kangaroos are more likely to groom themselves than to groom other kangaroos, mother kangaroos groom their young, and females in a mob sometimes groom each other. Grooming helps keep the animals clean and keeps the group together.

Take a Stand
Debate · *Research*

Should the Australian government ban the sale of kangaroo meat and other products?

The Australian government permits the harvesting of certain types of kangaroos where the animals are present in large numbers. Kangaroo meat, skins, and other products are then sold. Kangaroo meat is a popular food that is exported to more than 50 countries. Kangaroo skins are used to make shoes, car seats, and other products.

FOR

1. It is inhumane to kill kangaroos for the purpose of selling the meat and products made from the skins.
2. Once there is a worldwide market for kangaroo products, it may be hard to stop sales of the products even if the kangaroo population decreases.

AGAINST

1. Kangaroo products are made from only the most abundant species, so the sale of these products does not pose a threat to the overall kangaroo population.
2. The export of such products brings in millions of dollars each year, so it is good for the Australian **economy**.

Kangaroo
Connections

Kangaroo babies stay in their mother's pouch longer than any other marsupials.

Kangaroos raise more young that live to maturity than most other mammals do.

Mating and Birth

The larger types of kangaroos can breed at any time of the year, as long as enough food and water are present, although gray kangaroos tend to mate in spring and early summer. Once they reach about 2 years of age, female kangaroos spend most of their adult lives either pregnant or nursing a joey. Often, they do both at the same time, producing one joey after another if the conditions are right. Female kangaroos usually mate with dominant males. Females may prefer bigger males because their size indicates that they are strong survivors. A female kangaroo does not always mate with the same male. Instead, she mates with whichever male is dominant in the group at the time. In mobs, the old man kangaroo often chases away rival males.

Female kangaroos have pouches that open at the front, with four nipples inside for nursing their young. A female usually mates again shortly after she gives birth, when she has a small joey nursing in her pouch. After she mates, the fertilized egg that is created stops developing. It remains inside her womb until the joey leaves the pouch. Then, the fertilized egg begins to develop again, and a new joey will be born.

Kangaroos do not give birth if conditions are poor. For example, it would not be healthy for the mother or the joey if she gave birth during a **drought**. In dry times when there is not much green food for kangaroos to eat, females can put off giving birth. The joey will not begin to develop until certain chemicals, found in green food, let the mother's body know it is time for the joey to develop.

The **gestation period** for kangaroos is short compared to that of other mammals. Human babies stay in the womb for about 270 days before they are born. Kangaroos are in the womb for only 30 to 40 days. Once the joey is born, it must crawl to its mother's pouch within a few minutes. The mother helps the newborn by licking a path through her fur for the joey to follow.

Although the Goodfellow's tree kangaroo differs in appearance from larger kangaroos, the female cares for its young in much the same way.

Joeys

Kangaroo newborns are tiny and helpless. A newborn red or gray kangaroo may weigh less than 0.03 ounces (0.85 grams). Marsupial animals are born at a much less developed stage than cats, dogs, or humans. Most other mammal young spend months developing inside their mothers' bodies. In contrast, kangaroo young mostly develop outside their mother's body in the pouch. While joeys are developing in the pouch, most have an older brother or sister still nursing.

The bond between mother and joey grows as the joey develops enough to poke its way out of the pouch. When a foot, a tail, or a nose stick out, the mother sniffs and licks it. After a few months, the joey sticks its entire head out and inspects the world while its mother hops around. During this time, the joey depends on its mother for food, warmth, protection, and transportation. The mother carries the joey with her everywhere. Without her, it is unlikely the little kangaroo would survive. The mother is solely responsible for her joey. No other member of the mob, including the father, helps raise the joey.

At about 6 months old, as the joey gets bigger, it starts to leave the pouch for a few minutes at a time and begins to eat grass. By watching what its mother eats, the joey learns to forage, or search for food. Even as the joey continues to grow, it returns to its mother to nurse and receive comfort. By this time, it probably has a small brother or sister in the pouch. The mother produces two different types of milk, one for the new joey and one for the older joey that is spending more time out of the pouch.

Older joeys that are out of the pouch have to watch out for predators such as eagles, dingoes, large lizards, and snakes. If the mother spots danger, she warns the joey with a thump of her foot or a vocal sound. The joey dives back into the pouch. Sometimes, a female kangaroo is chased when she has a large joey in her pouch. If so, she may deliberately dump the joey out in tall grass or bushes where it can hide. She can then escape because she is able to run faster with a lighter load. If she is caught with a joey in her pouch, it is likely they would both die.

A mother kangaroo will not let her joey leave her pouch until she has checked the surroundings for danger.

Kangaroo
Connections

A joey is so firmly attached to its milk source during the first few months of life that it stays in place even when its mother is hopping about at a great speed.

Kangaroos are very productive breeders. If conditions are right, a kangaroo population can increase by four times in five years.

Development

Newborn kangaroos are blind, deaf, and hairless. Only the tiny head, shoulders, and forearms are formed. As soon as they are born, they must crawl up their mother's furry abdomen into the pouch. They use their arms like paddles through water to pull themselves into the pouch. This is a distance of about 6 inches (15.2 cm). If the tiny joey cannot find the pouch within a few minutes, it can die from exposure. The mother may lick a trail to the pouch, but she does not guide the joey in any other way. The joey is likely guided to the pouch by the smell of milk. Once in the pouch, the joey begins to nurse. It stays in this position for several months as it grows and develops.

Big changes begin for the joey when it is about 15 weeks old. The milk it drinks becomes richer, with more fat and protein, and the joey starts to grow. It grows a tail, and its claws become well formed. By 17 weeks of age, the joey's eyes have opened. The ears have opened as well, but they are folded back against the head. The joey is still pink-skinned and hairless for most of this time.

A joey can escape danger by diving headfirst into its mother's pouch. Then, it does a complete somersault to face the opening.

When the joey reaches 6 months of age, its mother's milk becomes even richer with a high fat content. By this time, the young kangaroo has a coat of fur and can better control its body temperature. The joey often sticks its head out of the pouch to look around. It starts to leave the pouch and may even nibble on grass as its mother grazes. Mother and joey start to form a close bond. The mother regularly cleans the pouch and joey by licking them.

By the time the joey is 9 months old, it can leave the pouch for longer periods of time and explore the outside world. The young kangaroo is curious and has much to learn. It watches its mother to see what grasses and other plants she eats. The joey also licks saliva from its mother's mouth, which helps them to bond. The mother's saliva also passes on tiny **bacteria** that help the joey digest green plant food. The joey still returns to the pouch for milk and comfort, but by the time it is 1 year old, it is too big for the pouch. Still, it sticks its head in the pouch for an occasional drink of milk.

By the time the young kangaroo reaches 18 months, it is no longer dependent on its mother. A young female may start to mate soon and have joeys of her own. Young males practice sparring with other young males. They need to grow larger and put on more weight before they can interest a female kangaroo as a mate.

Take a Stand
· Debate ·
· Research ·

Is it acceptable to remove problem animals in order to save kangaroos?

Many kangaroos are having a hard time surviving because of animals that have been introduced into Australia. Huge numbers of rabbits, mice, and goats eat kangaroo food and destroy their habitat. Some **feral** cats and foxes eat small kangaroos. Many solutions have been tried to get rid of these animals. Some of these involve trapping, shooting, or poisoning rabbits, foxes, and cats. Also, people have released diseased animals that pass along their illness to other animals of the same species.

FOR

1. These introduced animals are destroying Australia's natural wildlife heritage. If kangaroos become extinct, they will never return. Drastic methods must be used to save them.
2. Many of these pest animals, such as rabbits and mice, also destroy crops and pastures. The livelihoods of farmers have to be protected.

AGAINST

1. It is unacceptable to treat some animals inhumanely in order to protect others.
2. Some methods of removing pest animals, such as poisoning or disease, may affect kangaroos and other native animals in ways people do not yet understand.

Habitat

The continent of Australia has many different habitats, and kangaroos have spread out to occupy almost every type. Different types of kangaroos can be found in wooded forests and rainforests, on grassy plains, in arid scrublands, and even on rock walls. Tree kangaroos live in trees, while larger types of kangaroos take shelter under the trees, in caves, or in rock cliffs.

Kangaroos have a long history in Australia. While kangaroos are still found in every part of the country, they often now live in scattered pockets due to loss of habitat. Some of the large kangaroos have taken advantage of habitat changes made by humans and have expanded their range. The habitat of small kangaroos that dwell in the forest, however, is disappearing.

Organizing the Outback

Earth is home to millions of different **organisms**, all of which have specific survival needs. These organisms rely on their environment, or the place where they live, for their survival. All plants and animals have relationships with their environment. They interact with the environment itself, as well as the other plants and animals within the environment. These interactions create **ecosystems**.

Ecosystems can be broken down into levels of organization. These levels range from a single plant or animal to many species of plants and animals living together in an area.

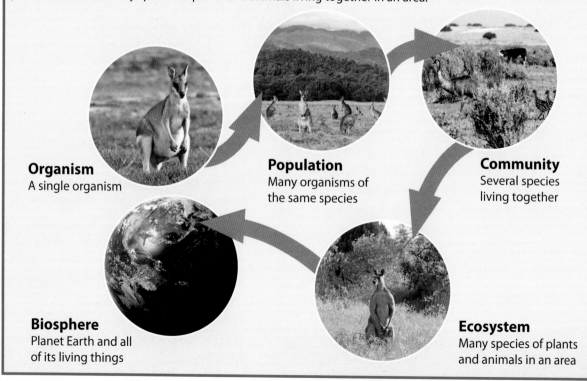

Organism
A single organism

Population
Many organisms of
the same species

Community
Several species
living together

Biosphere
Planet Earth and all
of its living things

Ecosystem
Many species of plants
and animals in an area

Kangaroo
Connections

Quokkas, which were once common in Australia, are now found in only a few areas. They can climb trees, which is unusual behavior for marsupials.

The quokka is the smallest type of wallaby. It favors moist, swampy areas.

Kangaroo Connections

The size of a kangaroo mob changes, depending on how much food is available and how good the food is.

To survive in a hot, dry environment, kangaroos are most active during the late afternoon, evening, and night. They avoid the daytime, when the temperature is highest.

Range

Different types of kangaroos live in all areas of Australia's mainland as well as the island of Tasmania, which is off the southern coast of Australia. Red kangaroos live in Australia's grasslands, plains, and deserts, where the land is flat and open. Both eastern and western gray kangaroos also inhabit the grasslands, as well as woodlands, and may live alongside red kangaroos. None of the large kangaroo species live in hilly or rocky areas, which are not suited to the way these animals move about. They also do not live in the continent's rainforests. Kangaroos spend the hottest part of the day resting in the shade. They are mainly active in the cooler evening and night.

Smaller species, such as the rock-wallabies and wallaroos, live in a variety of habitats, including wet forests and dry grasslands. These animals have shorter hind feet than the large kangaroos. This means that they can move about more easily in rocky places. It is hard to travel over long distances in these areas, so the **home range** of these species is relatively small. In contrast, a red kangaroo mob's home range can be as large as 1,600 acres (650 hectares). The home range of males is generally larger than that of females, and females tend to share their home range with other females. In general, kangaroos stay in one area unless there is a severe drought. If such a drought occurs, they travel to areas where they can find water and food.

Some species, such as quokkas, occupy small territories. They live in areas with a great deal of vegetation, where it is easier to find food. The range of a quokka may be as small as 5 acres (2 ha).

From an Expert

"If kangaroos are used for meat, for fur, for leather, then that's all people will see. People won't recognize their...value as wildlife, as animals in their own right beyond the realm of the human world. Everything is linked together, and if we damage this species we're damaging ourselves."
- Lynette Campbell

Lynette Campbell is a scientist who has been actively involved in the rescue, care, and release of orphaned joeys whose mothers have died as a result of hunting or car accidents. Her work was featured on the video "Kangaroos," which was part of the *Champions in the Wild* television series.

Diet

Kangaroos eat a variety of plants, such as leaves, grains, and fruits, but grasses are the plants most commonly eaten. Some of the smaller forest kangaroos are browsers. That means they eat leaves, twigs, and bark off trees and shrubs. To eat, they sit up and hold their food in their forepaws. Wallabies eat plants that grow in hilly areas and along rocks, and wallaroos eat spiky grasses.

Plant material, especially tough grasses, contains cellulose. This material, which makes plants stiff, is difficult to digest. Kangaroos have to eat a great deal of grass to survive because grass does not contain many nutrients. The animals have to break down the cellulose so that they can digest the food and get the maximum amount of energy from it. They eat slowly to be sure their food is finely ground before swallowing. When they swallow, the food goes to their stomach. Special bacteria in the stomach change the cellulose into a form that lets the kangaroos get the nutrients from the food.

Rat kangaroos, potoroos, and bettongs have different diets from larger kangaroos. Many of them eat mushrooms and other fungi. They also eat worms and insects.

Like all living things, kangaroos need water to survive. Kangaroos that live in dry areas may get all the water they need from the plants they eat. Many species have developed ways of saving water in their bodies. They do not sweat very much, and their urine and feces contain very little water. When water is scarce, some kangaroos dig deep holes that collect underground water. Also, animals that live on farmland often take advantage of water set out for sheep and cattle. In addition, some desert-dwelling rock-wallabies are so good at saving water in their bodies that they never need to drink. One species, the tammar wallaby, which lives on islands off the Australian coast, can drink seawater. Few other mammals can do this.

The Matschie's tree kangaroo eats mostly tree leaves. It also eats ferns, flowers, grass, moss, and bark.

Kangaroo
Connections

Kangaroos, like all macropods, have a stomach that is divided into chambers. The food they swallow can be brought back up from one chamber, chewed as cud, and then swallowed again to be digested.

Almost all of a kangaroo's waking hours are spent eating.

The Food Cycle

A food cycle shows how energy in the form of food is passed from one living thing to another. As kangaroos feed and move through their habitats, they affect the lives of the animals around them. The feeding habits of the kangaroos produce changes in the environment. In the diagram below, the arrows show the flow of energy from one living thing to another through a **food web**.

Secondary Consumers

Predators such as dingoes, Tasmanian devils, red foxes, and even eagles can prey on kangaroos. Joeys and smaller species are most at risk. Humans who eat kangaroo meat are also secondary consumers.

Primary Consumers

Kangaroos are herbivores that get energy from eating fungi and plants, such as grasses and shrubs. The large species of kangaroos graze on grass, biting off mouthfuls in much the same way that sheep do. Thin, sharp front teeth enable kangaroos to bite short grass.

Producers

Kangaroos get food energy from digesting the cellulose in the plants they eat. Feces from kangaroos can help spread plant seeds and fungi spores. This helps ensure a continuing food supply for kangaroos and other animals.

Decomposers

When kangaroos die, decomposers break down the animals' body materials, adding nutrients to the soil.

Parasites

Kangaroos provide a home for such parasites as nematode worms. The worms are found in a kangaroo's stomach and intestines.

Take a Stand
Debate • Research

Should the Australian government allow the taking of surplus kangaroos?

The Australian government allows the **culling** of kangaroos, in a program to contain overpopulation in certain areas. Hunters are allowed to target only specific types of kangaroos, in specific numbers.

FOR

1. There are strict controls on the hunting of kangaroos, which is allowed only according to the government's management program. The program poses no threat to the overall kangaroo population.
2. The kangaroo population has increased dramatically, and the animals may pose an environmental threat. They damage crops, and their overgrazing may put stress on the environment.

AGAINST

1. Kangaroos are part of the natural Australian ecosystem, and there is no evidence that they cause problems for the overall environment. In fact, they may be good for the ecosystem since their feeding on plants helps to control vegetation growth.
2. The culling program is expensive, and there are alternatives. Kangaroos have been successfully relocated from areas where they are present in large numbers to other places.

Kangaroo
Connections

Kangaroos can jump huge distances when moving fast but use very little energy while doing it. They are the only animals that use less energy the faster they travel.

Fast-traveling kangaroos remain in the air about 70 to 80 percent of the time.

Competition

In general, kangaroos are gentle creatures. This does not mean that there is no competition within a kangaroo mob. The kangaroos in a mob compete with each other for food, water, a shady resting place, and mates. The largest male is dominant in the group, but the younger, smaller males may try to challenge him.

The competition between males for females can be stiff, taking the form of sparring. The larger and more dominant boomers have the biggest selection of females for mating. Smaller or weaker males may not find a mate at all. The old man kangaroo may chase most or all rival males out of the group. When males spar, they sometimes use the sharp claws on their hind feet. A well-aimed kick using these claws can rip open the abdomen of an opponent. The skin on the abdomen of male kangaroos is thickened to provide protection. The play-sparring that joeys engage in helps them learn how to compete when they are older.

When a kangaroo mob grazes on a large area, there may be enough food so that members do not have to compete with one another. If food is scarce or found only in scattered areas, however, the animals do compete to get enough food. This can happen in a drought or after a fire. The kangaroos may compete over who gets to drink first at a water source or who gets the best shade spots if these are scarce.

Sparring matches between kangaroos do not usually last long. Often, the kangaroo being challenged backs down before the fight even begins.

Kangaroos with Other Animals

Although Tasmanian devils are only about the size of a dog, they attack and eat small kangaroos.

Even in Australia's wide open spaces, kangaroos find themselves in competition for food and places to live with many other creatures that share their habitat. In many areas, kangaroo habitats are shrinking because other species of animals are moving in. These other species are often animals introduced to Australia by humans, such as rabbits, mice, and goats. These animals often take over the habitats of kangaroos, eating their food and using or destroying their living spaces.

Kangaroos can also have problems with predators that have been brought to Australia by humans. The dingo was the first to arrive, about 3,000 years ago. Dingoes hunt kangaroos of most sizes. More recent arrivals that are causing serious problems for kangaroos are feral cats, dogs, and foxes. Small kangaroos are especially vulnerable to these predators. Small kangaroos also face danger from smaller marsupial predators, such as the Tasmanian devil.

Kangaroos also face threats from people. As more European settlers came to Australia over the past few hundred years, they increasingly affected the lives of kangaroos and other marsupials. Kangaroos had to share their food with animals that had been introduced by people. They also often became food for humans and certain introduced species. Humans hunt kangaroos for their meat and leather.

Kangaroos and humans experience the most conflict on farmlands, often when kangaroos compete for food with farmers' cattle and sheep. Humans have put up fences to protect their livestock, but kangaroos can jump over the fences. Humans often consider kangaroos to be pests that eat the grass needed for their sheep and cattle. Yet, researchers have found that kangaroos normally eat different grasses from the ones sheep prefer. Often, kangaroos and sheep can graze side by side without really competing. However, in times of drought, kangaroos have fewer food choices, and they can move in on grass intended for livestock.

Smaller kangaroos also have to compete with humans for living space. Many areas in which they live are being turned into housing developments, towns, and farms. As a result, many species of small kangaroos are being pushed out of their habitats. They are showing up in city parks and on suburban lawns.

Kangaroo Connections

Thirsty kangaroos have been known to dig holes 4 feet (1.2 m) deep to find water. Other animals then use these kangaroo-created wells to help them through the dry seasons.

Large kangaroos can go months without drinking water.

Folklore

Kangaroos have an important place in the legends and folklore of the Australian Aborigines. After they arrived in Australia about 40,000 to 50,000 years ago, Aborigines were the first people to encounter the continent's kangaroos. When European explorers first came to Australia in the 1600s and 1700s, they were amazed by these hopping creatures with their pouches and huge feet. It is said that the kangaroo received its name when baffled explorers asked an Aborigine what these creatures were. As the story goes, the Aborigine answered, *kangaroo*, which meant "I don't understand what you mean." The explorers took this to be the creature's name. Historians argue that there is no proof that this tale is true, but it is a part of the folklore surrounding kangaroos.

Kangaroos have appeared in the legends of the Australian people for thousands of years, and the stories have been told from one generation to another. One ancient Aboriginal legend tells of how the first kangaroos came to live in Australia. A huge windstorm blew strange-looking creatures through the air. The animals struggled to reach the ground. They stretched their legs so much that their back legs grew very long. When they finally dropped to the ground, they hopped away on their new long legs.

In the late 1800s and early 1900s, people sometimes put boxing gloves on male red or gray kangaroos and had them box humans. One early show featured "Jack the Fighting Kangaroo." The show was a popular attraction as it traveled throughout eastern Australia. Silent movies featuring boxing kangaroos were also popular. Most people now believe this activity was cruel. It used a kangaroo's natural behavior in a way that could cause the animal stress and injury. Still, even today, circuses and county fairs sometimes feature kangaroos taking part in "boxing matches" with people.

Boxing kangaroos were given to medal winners at an Australian sports competition. The boxing kangaroo is a national symbol of Australia.

Myth	**VS**	Fact
 The kangaroos in a mob all act the same way.		Scientists have observed kangaroos in a mob. The animals have been seen communicating and relating to each other, and they were all easily recognizable as unique individuals.
 Using a pouch to raise joeys is an inferior way of reproducing and caring for young.		Some researchers think that marsupial reproduction may be the best way to produce and raise young in the dry and often harsh conditions found in Australia.
 Large male kangaroos like to fight and are natural boxers.		Large male kangaroos do not look for fights with other animals and are not aggressive when left alone. They spar to compete with other kangaroos and to defend themselves against predators. They do not look for fights with other animals and are not aggressive when left alone.

Aboriginal rock paintings and drawings record stories and legends about kangaroos.

Logging in New Guinea has affected the habitat of tree kangaroos.

Animals on the Brink

Status

There are thought to be at least 54 species of kangaroos. At least seven species have become extinct in the past 200 years. Between 1880 and 1920, for example, the broad-faced potoroo and the eastern hare-wallaby became extinct. Then, in the 1930s, the toolache wallaby became extinct as well.

Many other kangaroo species, especially some of the smaller ones, are considered to have an uncertain chance of survival and could become extinct in the coming years. The International Union for Conservation of Nature (IUCN) publishes a "Red List" on the status of different species. The 2012 Red List stated that among marsupials in Australia, 13 species were critically **endangered**, the most serious status. In greatest danger are the tree kangaroos, which live in the rainforests of Australia as well as Indonesia and Papua New Guinea. Also in danger are hare-wallabies, nail-tail wallabies, some types of rock-wallabies, and many of the small forest species, such as quokkas, potoroos, and bettongs. In many cases, the habitats of these species have almost completely disappeared. Some of the larger species have done better, however. The gray and red kangaroos have actually grown in number and extended their range in some areas.

Some scientists believe that, in the future, climate change may pose a threat to kangaroos by affecting their habitats. They say that a rise in average temperatures could cause dry seasons to become hotter and rainfall to become more unpredictable. This could cause waterholes to dry up and grazing lands to disappear. These changes, in turn, could eventually lead to a shrinking of the areas in which kangaroos can live. According to some scientists, climate change could lead to the extinction of certain types of kangaroos such as the antilopine wallaroo. This animal favors a wet, tropical climate.

From an Expert

"The brush-tailed rock-wallaby's status is currently listed as threatened within New South Wales. Wallaby populations are being monitored on the mountain peaks at the Warrumbungle National Park [where] goats and foxes are potential threats.... This will [result] in the development of an improved recovery plan for the wallabies in the park." - Graeme Moss

Graeme Moss is a policy officer with the Department of Environment, Climate Change, and Water in New South Wales. He has taught wildlife ecology and has written articles on several kangaroo species, especially the red kangaroo.

Saving the Kangaroo

Kangaroos are well-known throughout the world. They are an important symbol of Australia, featured on the country's coat of arms, and tourists travel long distances to see them. All of Australia's states and territories have laws to protect kangaroos. Yet, the Australian government allows the hunting of certain types of kangaroos where they occur in large numbers. Even though kangaroos are protected from most hunting, the Environment Protection and Biodiversity Conservation Act 1999 outlines the ways that kangaroos can be hunted in the country. The government issues permits for the commercial harvesting of the red kangaroo, eastern gray kangaroo, western gray kangaroo, and common wallaroo, which is also called the euro.

In addition, different states and territories have kangaroo management plans that authorize the shooting of a specific number of kangaroos where there are thought to be too many. These kangaroos are said to put too much stress on the ecosystem. Under these programs, licensed "shooters" go out at night and hunt a predetermined number of kangaroos. Some people believe this is the best way to handle the kangaroos, while other people think that hunting kangaroos is an unwise practice.

Habitat loss poses another threat to kangaroos. The small brush fires that Aborigines often set in the past used to provide new habitat for kangaroos. These fires ensured that small areas of land would regenerate each year. There are now fewer of these small fires. This has led to an increase in the number of large and dangerous wildfires because of the build-up of brush in woodlands and forests.

Volunteers care for joeys who have become orphans because their mothers have been hunted or died in fires.

Large fires destroy too much kangaroo habitat, forcing the animals to travel far to find new places to live. Cars hit many kangaroos each year. Since light is low at dusk and dawn, it is difficult for drivers to see kangaroos on or beside roads. This makes the animals more vulnerable to being hit at these times.

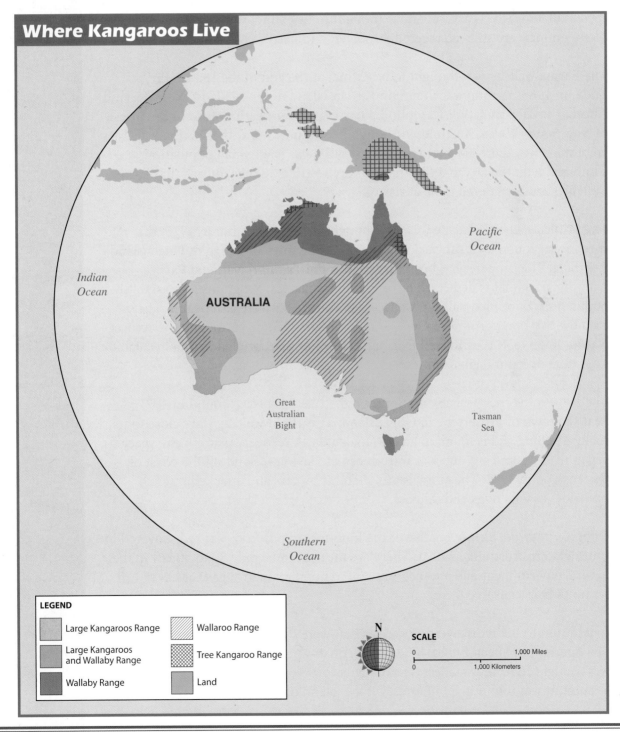

Where Kangaroos Live

Pacific Ocean

Indian Ocean

AUSTRALIA

Great Australian Bight

Tasman Sea

Southern Ocean

LEGEND

Large Kangaroos Range

Large Kangaroos and Wallaby Range

Wallaby Range

Wallaroo Range

Tree Kangaroo Range

Land

N

SCALE

0 — 1,000 Miles

0 — 1,000 Kilometers

Finding Extinct Species

Australia is a large country, and some kangaroo habitats fall within areas that are difficult for people to access. Many of the smaller species of kangaroos are secretive and protect themselves by hiding. In the late 20th century, some species of kangaroos that were once thought to be extinct were rediscovered. These animals are still endangered, however, and need to be protected.

The Parma wallaby was thought to be extinct at the end of the 18th century. Then, in 1965, a group was found on Kawau Island near Auckland, New Zealand. Another small population was found a few years later near Gosford in the forests of New South Wales, Australia. Although people now know that Parma wallabies are not extinct, there are very few of these animals. Their small population, combined with the fact that they have a very restricted range, means that Parma wallabies are considered to be at risk.

The bridled nail-tail wallaby was also thought to be extinct, but in 1973, the species was found by a kangaroo shooter near the town of Dingo in Queensland, Australia. The property has been turned into the Taunton National Park, a scientific park that is dedicated to preserving wallabies. Programs to reestablish populations of bridled nail-tail wallabies in other sites were also begun. There are now two other groups in Queensland at Idalia National Park and the Avocet Nature Reserve. It is estimated that only a few hundred bridled nail-tail wallabies exist in their natural environment.

The Proserpine rock-wallaby is another rediscovered species, found in 1977 near the town of Proserpine in Queensland. This timid wallaby stays close to its rocky dwelling and is found in a very small area. A recovery plan for the species began in 1991, and a group was introduced at Hayman Island off the coast of Queensland in 1998. The animals are often hit by cars and attacked by such predators as wild dogs and dingoes.

Gilbert's potoroo, a close relative of the long-footed potoroo, was rediscovered in southwestern Australia in 1994. There are thought to be only 30 to 40 left in their natural environment and another 40 to 50 in population groups that have been set up to help conserve them.

In addition to the rediscovery of species that were thought to be extinct, entirely new species have been found. In 2010, scientists announced the discovery of what was thought to be the smallest type of kangaroo ever, a dwarf wallaby the size of a rabbit. It was found in a rainforest on the island of New Guinea.

Parma wallabies once lived in forests along the Australian coast. As a result of human activity, they can no longer be found there.

Back from the Brink

Kangaroos and people have a long history together. Starting many thousands of years ago, Aborigines hunted kangaroos for food and hides. They knew much about the animals and how valuable they were. When European people came to Australia, they were fascinated by kangaroos. They also hunted the animals, which became an important part of their diet. Settlers, though, preferred to eat meat they were more familiar with, such as meat from cows and sheep. They introduced these types of livestock into Australia. Soon, kangaroos were viewed as pests that interfered with livestock. Today, some people still view kangaroos as pests. They support the Australian government's system of dealing with large numbers of kangaroos. People around the world also support the harvesting of kangaroos because they eat kangaroo meat and buy products made from kangaroo hides. There are many other people, however, who feel that there should be no such harvesting and hunting of kangaroos. They feel that kangaroos should be protected, and if the number of kangaroos is a problem, the animals should be relocated.

The larger types of kangaroos, including the red kangaroo and eastern and western gray kangaroos, are not considered at risk because there are so many of them. Other types of kangaroos are at risk, however, especially the smaller species. Many scientists feel that to protect Australia's biodiversity, all species of kangaroos must be preserved.

For more information about the Australian Wildlife Protection Council and its efforts to save kangaroos, contact:

**Australian Wildlife
Protection Council**
Kindness House
288 Brunswick Street, Suite 18
Fitzroy 3065 Victoria
Australia

Scientists know a great deal about the behavior of red and gray kangaroos, but the ways of other types of kangaroos are not as well understood.

Activity

Debating helps people think about ideas thoughtfully and carefully. When people debate, two sides take a different viewpoint on a subject. Each side takes turns presenting arguments to support its view.

Use the Take a Stand sections found throughout this book as a starting point for debate topics. Organize your friends or classmates into two teams. One team will argue in favor of the topic, and the other will argue against. Each team should research the issue thoroughly using reliable sources of information, including books, scientific journals, and trustworthy websites. Take notes of important facts that support your side of the debate. Prepare your argument using these facts to support your opinion.

During the debate, the members of each team are given a set amount of time to make their arguments. The team arguing the For side goes first. They have five minutes to present their case. All members of the team should participate equally. Then, the team arguing the Against side presents its arguments. Each team should take notes of the main points the other team argues.

After both teams have made their arguments, they get three minutes to prepare their rebuttals. Teams review their notes from the previous round. The teams focus on trying to disprove each of the main points made by the other team using solid facts. Each team gets three minutes to make its rebuttal. The team arguing the Against side goes first. Students and teachers watching the debate serve as judges. They should try to judge the debate fairly using a standard score sheet, such as the example below.

Criteria	Rate: 1-10	Sample Comments
1. Were the arguments well organized?	8	logical arguments, easy to follow
2. Did team members participate equally?	9	divided time evenly between members
3. Did team members speak loudly and clearly?	3	some members were difficult to hear
4. Were rebuttals specific to the other team's arguments?	6	rebuttals were specific, more facts needed
5. Was respect shown for the other team?	10	all members showed respect to the other team

2. What is the order of animals to which kangaroos belong?

3. How do kangaroos communicate that danger is present?

1. What is the largest species of kangaroo?

5. How do baby kangaroos develop soon after birth?

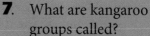

6. How fast can large kangaroos hop?

7. What are kangaroo groups called?

4. What is the average life span of a kangaroo living in nature?

9. What is the main reason that male kangaroos spar?

8. How many members of a kangaroo group help to raise a joey?

10. What are five predators that are a threat to kangaroos?

Answers:
1. red kangaroo 2. Diprotodontia, or marsupials 3. They thump their feet loudly and bang their tails on the ground. 4. 6 or 7 years 5. in their mother's pouch 6. 40 miles per hour (64 km per hour) 7. mobs 8. one, only the joey's mother 9. to compete over a female 10. dingoes, Tasmanian devils, foxes, eagles, and humans

Key Words

bacteria: microscopic, single-celled organisms

culling: to control the size of a group by removing some of its members

dingo: a species of wild dog found in Australia

dominant: stronger and more powerful than another animal

drought: a long period without rain

economy: the way a country manages its money and resources

ecosystems: communities of living things and resources

endangered: a type of plant or animal that exists in such small numbers that it is in danger of no longer surviving in the world

extinct: no longer surviving in the world

feral: a usually domestic animal, such as a dog or cat, that lives in nature and cares for itself

food web: connecting food chains that show how energy flows from one organism to another through diet

gestation period: the length of time that a female is pregnant

habitats: places where animals live, grow, and raise their young

herbivores: animals that prefer to eat plants

home range: the entire area in which a kangaroo group lives

mammals: warm-blooded animals that have hair or fur and nurse their young

mobs: groups of kangaroos that live together

order: one of eight major ranks used to classify animals, between class and family

organisms: forms of life

predators: animals that live by hunting other animals for food

scrubs: areas covered by small trees and bushes

sparring: hitting and pushing with forelegs in a way that resembles human boxing

species: groups of individuals with common characteristics

vocalizations: sounds that are made by animals

Index

Log on to www.av2books.com

AV² by Weigl brings you media enhanced books that support active learning. Go to www.av2books.com, and enter the special code found on page 2 of this book. You will gain access to enriched and enhanced content that supplements and complements this book. Content includes video, audio, weblinks, quizzes, a slide show, and activities.

AV² Online Navigation

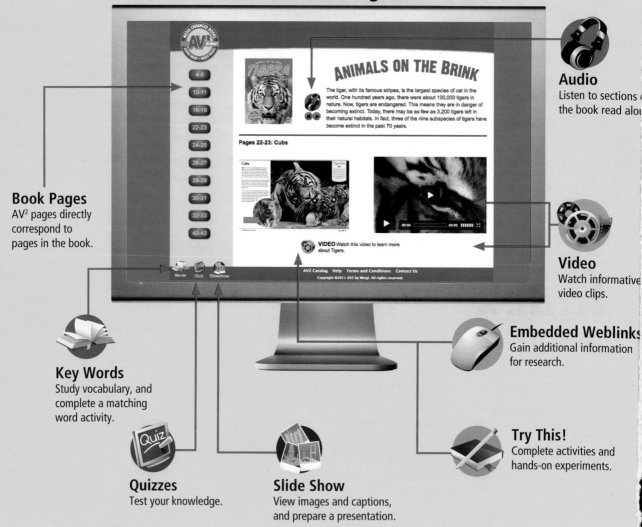

Audio
Listen to sections of the book read aloud

Book Pages
AV² pages directly correspond to pages in the book.

Video
Watch informative video clips.

Key Words
Study vocabulary, and complete a matching word activity.

Embedded Weblinks
Gain additional information for research.

Try This!
Complete activities and hands-on experiments.

Quizzes
Test your knowledge.

Slide Show
View images and captions, and prepare a presentation.

AV² was built to bridge the gap between print and digital. We encourage you to tell us what you like and what you want to see in the future.

Sign up to be an AV² Ambassador at www.av2books.com/ambassador.